KEVIN COSTNER

THE ALL-AMERICAN HERO:-FROM BASEBALL TO WESTERNS: KEVIN COSTNER'S JOURNEY THROUGH HOLLYWOOD

JESSIE G. BECK

TABLE OF CONTENTS

INTRODUCTION

American actor, producer, and director of motion pictures is Kevin Michael Costner. A Primetime Emmy, two Screen Actors Guild Awards, three Golden Globe Awards, two Academy Awards, and more honors have been bestowed upon him. Costner was raised in Compton, California, after being born in Lynwood, California, on January 18, 1955. Sharon Costner and William Costner were his parents. Of the three sons, he is the youngest; the other two passed away at birth. William Costner was an electrician and utilities executive, and Sharon Rae Costner (née Tedrick) worked in welfare.. Costner's father's heritage originates with German immigrants to North Carolina in the 1700s, and Costner also has English, Irish, Scottish, and Welsh ancestry. Costner was raised Baptist. He was not academically inclined in school, but did play sports (especially football), take piano lessons, write poetry, and sing in the First Baptist Choir. He has said that watching the 1962 film How the West Was Won as a child inspired his love for Western films.

According to Costner, as his father's profession developed, he moved around California during his adolescent years. He has stated that he "lost a lot of confidence" at this time and frequently had to establish new pals. After moving to Visalia, Costner resided in Ventura. Costner was in the marching band at Mt. Whitney High School. In 1973, Costner received his diploma from Villa Park High School. He and Dennis Burtt were teammates at Villa Park, where he played baseball. California State University, Fullerton (CSUF) awarded him a bachelor's degree. He joined the Delta Chi fraternity at CSUF and was initiated as a brother.

Costner became interested in acting and dancing while in his last year of college. In 1978, while on an airplane returning from his honeymoon in Puerto Vallarta, Costner had a chance encounter with actor Richard Burton. At that time, Costner was uncertain about whether he should become an actor, and he approached Burton to ask his advice. Costner has said that Burton encouraged him to pursue acting. Costner has also stated that he asked Burton whether it was possible to be an actor without experiencing turmoil in one's private life; according to Costner, Burton replied that he thought it was possible. Costner credits Burton with inspiring him to become an actor.

Having agreed to undertake a job as a marketing executive, Costner began taking acting lessons five nights a week, with the support of his wife. His marketing job lasted 30 days. He took work which allowed him to develop his acting skills via tuition, including working on fishing boats, as a truck driver, and giving tours of stars' Hollywood homes to support the couple while he also attended auditions.

Tribute To Kevin Costner

Kevin Costner is a legendary character in American film, one whose name conjures up a picture of legendary performances, directing coups, and a steadfast devotion to his art. From his modest beginnings as a young, talented actor to his rise to prominence in Hollywood, Costner's life story is a monument to his skill, tenacity, and unshakable faith in the power of narrative.

A number of Costner's works have altered the direction of American filmmaking, leaving an indelible mark on his career. He brought Eliot Ness to life in "The Untouchables," the film about the uncorruptible lawman fighting against the evil of Prohibition. With "Field of Dreams," he composed a classic hymn to dreams, baseball, and the everlasting value of companionship. Additionally, he explored the wild American West in "Dances with Wolves," crafting a masterpiece of film that won over hearts all over the world.

In addition to his skill as an actor, Costner has established himself as a visionary producer, director, and storyteller. After taking over "Dances with Wolves," he led the movie to seven Academy Awards, including Best Picture and Best Director, as well as critical acclaim. He brought life back to the Western genre with "Open

Range," honoring the cinematic traditions he held in such high regard. Additionally, he brought to life the fabled conflict between two families in the epic television miniseries "Hatfields & McCoys," telling a story of love, grief, and the lingering influence of the past.

Costner has made significant contributions outside of the movie industry. He has made a name for himself as a philanthropist by giving his time and money to a range of causes, such as veterans' affairs, education, and environmental protection. His steadfast dedication to contributing to society is indicative of his sincere empathy and aspiration to have a constructive influence on the world.

Kevin Costner leaves behind a legacy of unrelenting devotion to his art, a profound love of narrative, and a resolve to use his position to change the world for the better. He is a genuine American legend who serves as motivation for young filmmakers and storytellers as well as a reminder that the magic of movies rests in their capacity to enthrall, inspire, and unite us.

CHAPTER 1: EARLY LIFE AND CAREER

Early Life and Career: From Humble Beginnings to Hollywood Stardom

Kevin Costner's journey to Hollywood stardom was a path paved with perseverance, talent, and a touch of serendipity. Born in Lynwood, California on January 18, 1955, Costner's early life was marked by frequent relocations due to his father's job as an electrician. This nomadic existence instilled in him a sense of adaptability and a keen observation of people from diverse backgrounds.

Costner's passion for storytelling emerged early on. He excelled in writing classes and participated in school plays. Despite his academic struggles, he possessed a natural charisma and a captivating stage presence. After graduating from Villa Park High School in 1973, Costner enrolled at California State University, Fullerton, where he initially majored in business.

However, Costner's true calling beckoned. During his college years, he developed a growing interest in acting and began taking classes at the Orange County Community College. His dedication to his craft was unwavering, often taking acting lessons five nights a week while juggling his academic and personal commitments.

In 1978, Costner graduated from CSUF with a business degree, but his heart remained set on acting. He moved to Hollywood, embarking on a journey that would transform him into one of the most celebrated figures in American cinema.

Costner's early acting career was marked by small roles and challenging auditions. He worked various jobs to make ends meet, including driving a truck and marketing surfboards. But he never lost sight of his dream, continuing to pursue acting opportunities with unwavering determination.

His breakthrough came in 1985 with the Western film "Silverado," where he played Jake Sullivan, a courageous and loyal cowboy. While his scenes were initially cut, his performance caught the attention of director Lawrence Kasdan, who cast him in the 1987 film "The Untouchables."

In "The Untouchables," Costner portrayed Eliot Ness, the incorruptible lawman determined to bring down Al Capone's criminal empire. His portrayal of Ness was both powerful and nuanced, establishing him as a leading man in Hollywood.

Costner's star continued to rise with a series of critically acclaimed films, including "Bull Durham" (1988), "Field of Dreams" (1989), and "Dances with Wolves" (1990). These films showcased his versatility as an actor, seamlessly transitioning from charismatic baseball player to idealistic farmer to Civil War soldier who befriends a Lakota Sioux tribe.

In 1990, Costner's directorial debut, "Dances with Wolves," cemented his status as a Hollywood icon. The film, set in the American West, explored themes of cultural understanding, friendship, and the preservation of wilderness. It garnered seven Academy Awards, including Best Picture and Best Director, solidifying Costner's position as a visionary filmmaker.

Costner's journey from humble beginnings to Hollywood stardom is a testament to his unwavering dedication to his craft, his innate talent, and his ability to connect with audiences on a profound level. He is a true American icon, a master storyteller who has enriched the cinematic landscape with his captivating performances and visionary filmmaking.

Sustaining Success and Expanding Horizons

Despite facing occasional critical and commercial setbacks, Kevin Costner's career has remained remarkably resilient, spanning over four decades. He has consistently reinvented himself, taking on diverse roles and exploring new genres, proving his adaptability and range as an actor.

In the 1990s, Costner continued to take on challenging roles, portraying complex characters in films such as "JFK" (1991), "The Bodyguard" (1992), and "Robin Hood: Prince of Thieves" (1991). These films showcased his versatility and willingness to push boundaries, further cementing his reputation as a leading man.

Despite the financial struggles faced by his production company, Tig Productions, Costner remained undeterred. He continued to pursue ambitious projects, including the post-apocalyptic epic "The Postman" (1997) and the historical drama "Thirteen Days" (2000). While these films received mixed reviews, they demonstrated Costner's unwavering commitment to storytelling and his willingness to take creative risks.

In the early 2000s, Costner ventured into the realm of television, starring in the acclaimed miniseries "Hatfields & McCoys" (2012). His portrayal of Anse Hatfield earned him critical praise and an Emmy Award, showcasing his ability to captivate audiences on both the big and small screens.

Throughout his career, Costner has consistently demonstrated a deep respect for the craft of filmmaking. He has collaborated with talented directors, writers, and fellow actors, creating films that have resonated with audiences worldwide.

A Legacy of Inspiration and Philanthropic Endeavors

Kevin Costner's legacy extends far beyond his cinematic achievements. He has established himself as a role model for aspiring filmmakers and a respected figure in the entertainment industry. His unwavering dedication to his craft, his willingness to take creative risks, and his genuine passion for storytelling have inspired countless individuals to pursue their own dreams.

Beyond his acting and filmmaking contributions, Costner has also made significant philanthropic contributions. He is a passionate advocate for environmental protection, supporting organizations dedicated to preserving wilderness and promoting sustainable practices. He has also established the Kevin Costner & Lynn Spielberg Family Foundation, which provides support for educational and arts initiatives.

Costner's commitment to giving back to society exemplifies his genuine compassion and desire to make a positive impact on the world. He understands that his platform as a successful actor and filmmaker carries with it a responsibility to use his influence to make a difference.

An Enduring Icon

Kevin Costner's journey from humble beginnings to Hollywood stardom is a testament to his perseverance, talent, and unwavering commitment to his craft. He has proven himself to be a master storyteller, a gifted actor, and a visionary filmmaker, leaving an indelible mark on the cinematic landscape.

His legacy is one of inspiration, creativity, and social responsibility. He has shown that it is possible to achieve great things while remaining true to one's values and using one's talents to make a positive impact on the world. Kevin Costner is a true American icon, a symbol of hard work, dedication, and the power of storytelling to connect us all.

The Birth of a Star: Kevin Costner's Journey to Stardom

Kevin Costner's rise to stardom is a tale of perseverance, talent, and the unwavering pursuit of a dream. Born in Lynwood, California, on January 18, 1955, Costner's childhood was marked by frequent relocations, a result of his father's job as an electrician. This nomadic existence instilled in him a sense of adaptability and a keen observation of people from diverse backgrounds.

Despite his academic struggles, Costner displayed a natural charisma and a captivating stage presence. After graduating from Villa Park High School in 1973, he enrolled at California State University, Fullerton, initially majoring in business. However, Costner's true calling beckoned.

During his college years, Costner developed a growing interest in acting and began taking classes at the Orange County Community College. His dedication to his craft was unwavering, often taking acting lessons five nights a week while juggling his academic and personal commitments.

In 1978, Costner graduated from CSUF with a business degree, but his heart remained set on acting. He moved to Hollywood, embarking on a journey that would transform him into one of the most celebrated figures in American cinema.

Costner's early acting career was marked by small roles and challenging auditions. He worked various jobs to make ends meet, including driving a truck and marketing surfboards. But he never lost sight of his dream, continuing to pursue acting opportunities with unwavering determination.

His breakthrough came in 1985 with the Western film "Silverado," where he played Jake Sullivan, a courageous and loyal cowboy. While his scenes were initially cut, his performance caught the attention of director Lawrence Kasdan, who cast him in the 1987 film "The Untouchables."

In "The Untouchables," Costner portrayed Eliot Ness, the incorruptible lawman determined to bring down Al Capone's criminal empire. His portrayal of Ness was both powerful and nuanced, establishing him as a leading man in Hollywood.

Costner's star continued to rise with a series of critically acclaimed films, including "Bull Durham" (1988), "Field of Dreams" (1989), and "Dances with Wolves" (1990). These films showcased his versatility as an actor, seamlessly transitioning from charismatic baseball player to idealistic farmer to Civil War soldier who befriends a Lakota Sioux tribe.

In 1990, Costner's directorial debut, "Dances with Wolves," cemented his status as a Hollywood icon. The film, set in the American West, explored themes of cultural understanding, friendship, and the preservation of wilderness. It garnered seven Academy Awards, including Best Picture and Best Director, solidifying Costner's position as a visionary filmmaker.

Throughout his career, Costner has consistently demonstrated a deep respect for the craft of filmmaking. He has collaborated with talented directors, writers, and fellow actors, creating films that have resonated with audiences worldwide.

Costner's journey from humble beginnings to Hollywood stardom is a testament to his unwavering dedication to his craft, his innate talent, and his ability to connect with audiences on a profound level. He is a true American icon, a master storyteller who has enriched the cinematic landscape with his captivating performances and visionary filmmaking.

From Marketing to Acting: Kevin Costner's Unexpected Career Shift

Kevin Costner's journey to Hollywood stardom stands as a testament to the power of following one's dreams, even when it means taking an unexpected turn. Unlike many aspiring actors who set out with a clear vision of their artistic path, Costner's journey began in a seemingly unrelated field: marketing.

After graduating with a business degree from California State University, Fullerton, Costner embarked on a career in marketing, working for various companies in the Los Angeles area. While his marketing skills were undoubtedly valuable, Costner couldn't shake off the persistent call of acting that had been tugging at him since his college days.

Driven by an innate passion for storytelling and a desire to perform, Costner began taking acting classes in his spare time. He juggled his marketing job with acting lessons, often taking classes late at night or on weekends. His dedication was unwavering, fueled by a belief in his untapped potential.

Despite the challenges of pursuing two demanding careers simultaneously, Costner's perseverance paid off. In 1978, he landed his first significant acting role in a small independent film called "Sizzlin' Surfers." This small role opened doors to more opportunities, and Costner gradually transitioned from marketing to acting full-time.

In the early 1980s, Costner began appearing in supporting roles in various films and television shows. He played minor characters in films such as "Night Shift" (1982) and "Testament" (1983), slowly gaining experience and honing his craft.

A pivotal moment in Costner's career arrived in 1985 with the Western film "Silverado." Although his scenes were initially cut from the final edit, his performance caught the attention of director Lawrence Kasdan, who was impressed by his raw talent and screen presence.

Kasdan cast Costner in the lead role of Eliot Ness in the 1987 film "The Untouchables." Costner's portrayal of the incorruptible lawman battling Al Capone's criminal empire was both powerful and nuanced, establishing him as a leading man in Hollywood.

With his star on the rise, Costner went on to deliver a string of critically acclaimed performances in films such as "Bull Durham" (1988), "Field of Dreams" (1989), and "Dances with Wolves" (1990). These films showcased his versatility as an actor, seamlessly transitioning from charismatic baseball player to idealistic farmer to Civil War soldier who befriends a Lakota Sioux tribe.

Costner's journey from marketing to acting is a remarkable tale of unexpected career shifts and unwavering determination. He dared to follow his passion, even when it meant navigating an unconventional path. His story serves as an inspiration to aspiring actors and individuals from all walks of life, demonstrating that with dedication and perseverance, dreams can indeed become reality.

Kevin Costner's Journey to Hollywood Stardom: A Tale of Perseverance and Passion

Kevin Costner's rise to Hollywood stardom is a testament to the power of perseverance, talent, and an unwavering belief in one's dreams. Unlike many aspiring actors who embark on their journey with a clear vision of their artistic path, Costner's route to stardom was far from straightforward.

After graduating from California State University, Fullerton, with a business degree, Costner initially pursued a career in marketing. However, the allure of acting never left him. He continued to take acting classes in his spare time, juggling his marketing job with acting lessons late at night or on weekends.

Costner's dedication to his craft paid off. In 1978, he landed his first significant acting role in a small independent film called "Sizzlin' Surfers." This small role opened doors to more opportunities, and Costner gradually transitioned from marketing to acting full-time.

The early 1980s saw Costner appearing in supporting roles in various films and television shows. He played minor characters in films such as "Night Shift" (1982) and "Testament" (1983), slowly gaining experience and honing his craft.

A pivotal moment in Costner's career arrived in 1985 with the Western film "Silverado." Although his scenes were initially cut from the final edit, his performance caught the attention of director Lawrence Kasdan, who was impressed by his raw talent and screen presence.

Kasdan cast Costner in the lead role of Eliot Ness in the 1987 film "The Untouchables." Costner's portrayal of the incorruptible lawman battling Al Capone's criminal empire was both powerful and nuanced, establishing him as a leading man in Hollywood.

With his star on the rise, Costner went on to deliver a string of critically acclaimed performances in films such as "Bull Durham" (1988), "Field of Dreams" (1989), and "Dances with Wolves" (1990). These films showcased his versatility as an actor, seamlessly transitioning from charismatic baseball player to idealistic farmer to Civil War soldier who befriends a Lakota Sioux tribe.

Costner's journey to Hollywood stardom is a remarkable tale of unexpected career shifts and unwavering determination. He dared to follow his passion, even when it meant navigating an unconventional path. His story serves as an inspiration to aspiring actors and individuals from all walks of life, demonstrating that with dedication and perseverance, dreams can indeed become reality.

CHAPTER 2: CAREER

1981–1986: Rise To Prominence

Sizzle Beach, U.S.A. was Costner's first motion picture
(1981). The picture was not released until 1981 and was
re-released in 1986. It was shot throughout the winter of
1978–79. Many people mistakenly believed that Costner
had his film debut in 1983's The Touch (also known as
Stacy's Knights), starring Eve Lilith and Andra Millian,
due to release issues and a dearth of supporting
material.[Reference required] Costner was "Frat Boy #1"
in a small part in the 1982 Ron Howard picture Night
Shift. He makes an appearance at the pinnacle of a
blow-out party at the New York City morgue, where a
furious Henry Winkler abruptly stops the music. Holding

a beer, Costner appears shocked by the abrupt end of the festivities.

Costner appeared in a commercial for the Apple Lisa and Table for Five in 1983, and, the same year, had a small role in the nuclear holocaust film Testament. Later, he was cast in The Big Chill and filmed several scenes that were planned as flashbacks, but they were removed from the final cut. His role was that of Alex, the friend who committed suicide, the event that brings the rest of the cast together. Costner was a friend of director Lawrence Kasdan, who promised the actor a role in a future project. That became Silverado (1985) and a breakout role for Costner. He also starred that year in the smaller films Fandango and American Flyers and appeared alongside Kiefer Sutherland in an hour-long special episode of Steven Spielberg's Amazing Stories.

1987–1994: Stardom and acclaim

When Costner played federal agent Eliot Ness in The Untouchables and the title role in the thriller No Way Out in 1987, he became a Hollywood celebrity. His roles in the baseball-themed movies Field of Dreams (1989) and Bull Durham (1988) cemented his place on the A-list. He founded Tig Productions in 1990 as a joint venture with producer Jim Wilson. The epic Dances with Wolves, which Costner both directed and acted in, was Tig's debut feature. Twelve Academy Awards were received for this movie, and it took home seven of them, including two for him directly (Best Picture and Best Director). The same year saw the release of Revenge, a Tony Scott-directed film in which he acted alongside Anthony Quinn and Madeleine Stowe; Costner had always wanted to direct it himself.

Costner portrayed Robin Hood in the action-adventure film Robin Hood: Prince of Thieves (1991) where he also served as a producer. Costner starred alongside Alan Rickman, Morgan Freeman, and Christian Slater. The film received mixed reviews but was an immense box-office success. He then starred as District Attorney Jim Garrison in the Oliver Stone-directed political epic thriller JFK (1991). The film gained significant controversy for its historical inaccuracies but was also praised for its style, direction, and performances. Costner received a Golden Globe Award for Best Actor – Motion Picture Drama nomination for his role. Critic Roger Ebert praised his performance writing, "As Garrison, Costner gives a measured yet passionate performance. Like a man who has hold of an idea he cannot let go, he forges ahead, insisting that there is more to the assassination than meets the eye."

Later, he produced and appeared alongside Whitney Houston in the romance drama The Bodyguard (1992). The movie was both a commercial and cultural success. He played a convict on the run in Clint Eastwood's drama A Perfect World (1993) the following year. "Costner seems about as pathological as a koala bear, and his gentle charisma reinforces the film's touchy-feely theme," Entertainment Weekly film critic Owen

Gleiberman observed.[9][26] In the 1994 Lawrence Kasdan-directed western biopic Wyatt Earp, he played the lead role and produced the film. He starred in the drama picture The War that same year. Elijah Wood costarred in the movie as well. The movie didn't appear to get much notice.

1995–2011: Career fluctuation

The science fiction-post-apocalyptic epics Waterworld (1995) and The Postman (1997), the latter of which Costner also directed, were both commercial disappointments and both largely regarded by critics as artistic failures. However, while Waterworld achieved respectable box office and some positive reviews, results for The Postman were far worse and it ended up winning five Golden Raspberry Awards, including Worst Picture, Worst Actor and Worst Director for Costner. Costner starred in the golf comedy Tin Cup (1996) for Ron Shelton, who had previously directed him in Bull

Durham. He developed the film Air Force One and was set to play the lead role of the President, but ultimately decided to concentrate on finishing The Postman instead. He personally offered the project to Harrison Ford. In 1999, he starred in Message in a Bottle with Robin Wright, based on the novel of the same name by Nicholas Sparks. The film drew mixed reviews and just about broke even at the box office.

In the 2000 film Thirteen Days, he played John F. Kennedy's top adviser Kenneth O'Donnell, which helped him slightly restore his career. He directed and starred in the western Open Range, which was a surprising economic success in 2003 in addition to receiving critical acclaim. In The Upside of Anger, he played retired professional baseball player Denny Davies, earning him some of his best praise. For this part, he earned the San Francisco Film Critics Circle Award for Best Supporting Actor and was nominated by the Broadcast Film Critics Association. Following that, Costner played a serial killer in the films Mr. Brooks and

The Guardian. His Tig Productions business collapsed in 2008, and it was renamed Tree House Films.

In 2008, Costner starred in Swing Vote. He starred opposite Jennifer Aniston in the 2005 movie Rumour Has It. Costner was honored on September 6, 2006, when his hand and foot prints were set in concrete in front of Grauman's Chinese Theatre alongside those of other celebrated actors and entertainers. In 2010, he appeared in The Company Men alongside Ben Affleck, Tommy Lee Jones and Chris Cooper. It debuted at the Sundance Film Festival, and received good reviews. It was released in cinemas worldwide in January 2011. The film was considered to be an Oscar contender, but did not get a nomination.

Costner announced that he would be returning to the director's chair for the first time in seven years, in 2011, with A Little War of Our Own. He was also about to team up again with director Kevin Reynolds in Learning Italian. No updates have been released about either film since their original production announcement. He also appears, as a special cameo, in Funny or Die's "Field of Dreams 2: NFL Lockout". Costner portrayed Jonathan Kent in the rebooted Superman film Man of Steel, directed by Zack Snyder. Costner was going to have a role in Quentin Tarantino's Django Unchained, but had to drop out due to scheduling conflicts.

2012–present: Resurgence And Yellowstone

In the three-part miniseries Hatfields & McCoys, which debuted on the History Channel on May 28, 2012, Costner played Devil Anse Hatfield. It attracted 13.9 million viewers, smashing the record. The miniseries narrates the authentic American tale of a fabled family conflict that lasted for several decades and almost resulted in a war between West Virginia and Kentucky. Costner won the 2013 Screen Actors Guild Award for Outstanding Performance by a Male Actor in a Miniseries or Television Movie, the 2013 Golden Globe

Award for Best Performance by an Actor in a Limited Series or a Motion Picture Made for Television, and the 2012 Emmy Award for Outstanding Lead Actor in a Miniseries or Movie for his role.

In 2014, Costner appeared in the spy movie Jack Ryan: Shadow Recruit, as Thomas Harper, a mentor for the series' title character. The same year, he starred in the thriller 3 Days to Kill and the drama Draft Day and produced and starred in Black or White. Black or White premiered at the 2014 Toronto International Film Festival and opened in the United States in 2015. In 2015, Costner played coach Jim White in the drama film McFarland, USA, about cross-country running. In 2016, he played the fictional character Al Harrison, a NASA Space Task Group supervisor, in Hidden Figures, and in 2017, he starred with Jessica Chastain in Aaron Sorkin's directorial debut film Molly's Game. Since 2018, he has starred in and produced the television series Yellowstone, marking the first regular TV series role of his career. In 2019, Costner starred in The Art of Racing in the Rain, where he voiced Enzo the dog. It was his first voice-over film in his career.

In August 2022, Costner began production on Horizon: An American Saga, a Western epic that will be split into at least four films, each just under three hours in length. Costner plans on the films being released over a series of months. Costner will act as director of the project and said the film was proposed as an event television series. Production on the first film was expected to last at least 220 days, but was completed by November 2022. Production of the next films was underway by May 2023.

CHAPTER 3:OTHER VENTURES

With the support of his wife Christine, Costner formed the country rock group Kevin Costner & Modern West, of which he is the lead vocalist. They started a global tour in October 2007 that included performances in Rome and Istanbul. Additionally, the trio appeared at races for the NASCAR Sprint Cup Series at Charlotte Motor Speedway in Concord, North Carolina, and Daytona International Speedway.

On November 11, 2008, the group's country album Untold Truths was released by Universal South Records. The album reached at No. 35 on the Top Heatseekers list and No. 61 on the Billboard Top Country Albums. None of the three radio-released singles—"Superman 14," "Long Hot Night," and "Backyard"—have charted. A live music video for the single "Superman 14" was produced.

In 2009, they went on tour with opening act The Alternate Routes. In August, at the Big Valley Jamboree in Camrose, Alberta, Costner and the band were scheduled next on stage when a severe thunderstorm struck, causing the stage and stands on the main stage to collapse. One person was reported dead and forty injured. Later, an auction was held to raise money for the two young sons of the woman killed. A dinner with Costner was auctioned off for $41,000. Two guitars, one autographed by Costner, helped raise another $10,000 each.

A second Kevin Costner and Modern West album, Turn It On, was released in February 2010 in Europe and was supported by a European tour. In July 2012, the band performed in Halifax, Nova Scotia, at the 20th annual Telus World Skins Game in support of the IWK Health Centre Foundation, donating a guitar autographed by Costner.

Additionally, Kevin Costner made an appearance in Marieke Schröder's documentary film Country Roads.

Tales from Yellowstone, the most recent CD by Kevin Costner and Modern West, was written by Costner and his co-writers from the viewpoint of John Dutton, who was played by Costner in the popular television series Yellowstone. Season 3 of the show included songs from the album.

Baseball

In Chasing Dreams, Bull Durham, Field of Dreams, For Love of the Game, and The Upside of Anger, among other movies, Costner has portrayed a professional baseball player in three of the films and a former professional baseball player in another.

Austin, Texas, is home to Costner, who occasionally shows up to Texas Longhorns baseball workouts and games. During Augie Garrido's time as a baseball coach at Costner's alma mater, Cal State Fullerton, he was a close buddy of the former Longhorns coach. In For Love of the Game, he tapped Garrido to play the Yankee manager. He makes an effort to get to every College World Series game in Omaha, Nebraska, where the CSUF Titans play. Although Costner showed up for a tryout, he was not selected for the squad in his first year of college.

Costner owned a portion of the independent baseball team Lake County Fielders in the North American League, which is situated in Zion, Illinois. On August 12, 2021, he led the New York Yankees and Chicago White Sox onto the field prior to the MLB at Field of Dreams game held in Dyersville, Iowa and gave a short speech.

Commercial Objectives

Costner acquired a company in 1995 that was creating oil separation devices using a patent he had acquired from the US government. The company's creations had limited commercial value prior to the Deepwater Horizon oil spill, when BP removed six of the devices for testing in late May 2010 from Ocean Therapy Solutions, a business in which Costner had a stake. 32 of the oil-water separation devices were leased by BP from Ocean Therapy Solutions on June 16, 2010. Spyron Contoguris and Stephen Baldwin filed a case in Louisiana District Court, claiming $10.64 million for securities fraud and deception, despite having previously sold their stakes in Ocean Therapy Solutions to another investor in the company in mid-June. The suit claimed that Costner kept a meeting with BP secret from them, and the secret meeting resulted in an $18-million down payment on a $52 million purchase, and that after the down payment, but before any announcement, another investor used part of the down payment to buy out their shares, thus excluding them from their share of the profits from the total sale. The lawsuit asserted that Baldwin and Contogouris were informed that BP was still testing the machines and had not yet committed to leasing the machines from Ocean Therapy Solutions, and that the other investor in Ocean Therapy Solutions had

bought their shares for $1.4 million to Baldwin and
$500,000 to Contogouris, in spite of public statements
made to the contrary by Costner, Ocean Therapy
Solutions, BP, and others. In the multimillion-dollar
oil-clean-up case, a federal jury in Louisiana deliberated
for less than two hours in June 2012 before rejecting the
claims of Baldwin and Contogouris. The court then
ordered Baldwin and Contogouris to compensate Costner
and the other defendants in the case for their costs.

One mile south of Deadwood, South Dakota, on U.S.
Route 85, Costner opened Tatanka: The Story of the
Bison on June 6, 2004, expressing his desire that it
would serve as a poignant and instructive resource for
anyone learning about America's westward development.
The $5 million attraction, according to promoters, has a
brand-new 3,800-square-foot interactive center with
displays, shops, and food and drink sections in addition
to offices and a small theater. The visitor center has text
and images about the bison and the Plains Indians'
relationship to them, including how they used to hunt
them and now raise them for clothes and food. The focal

point is a bronze sculpture of a buffalo jump by Hill City artist Peggy Detmers, which shows three bronze Lakota riders riding horses and fourteen bronze bison fleeing from their attackers. Three enormous bison are positioned to fall over a precipice in a graceful stance. Detmers was commissioned by Costner in 1994. At Eagle Bronze Foundry in Lander, Wyoming, five-fourths-scale bronze sculptures weighing between 2,500 and 8,000 pounds were cast.

In Deadwood, South Dakota, Costner opened the Midnight Star Casino and Restaurant in 1991. He paid salary and bonuses to Francis and Carla Caneva, who he hired to run the business and gave each a 3.25 percent ownership stake in it. In July 2004, he asked to agree to an amicable disassociation and ended their job. Costner engaged an accountant to establish the partnership's fair market value, and after they declined, he dissolved it and took $3.1 million. Costner was sued by the Canevas, who demanded that he either acquire their shares for double that sum or sell the business on the open market. They prevailed in the lower court but lost before the

South Dakota Supreme Court because to Costner's appeal. Costner sold the business in 2020 after closing it in 2017.

In 2020, Costner became an investor, podcast narrator, and co-founder of Woody Sears's new audio entertainment travel app, HearHere. When visitors take road excursions across the United States and wish to learn about the people, places, and histories they are experiencing along the way, Costner narrates a few of the audio stories offered by the iPhone subscription app.

Philanthropy

Costner is a member of the National World War I Museum's honorary board in Kansas City, Missouri. He taped two radio ads for the museum that were broadcast on the Kansas City Royals Radio Network in the spring of 2011.

NASCAR

The Auto Club 500 of the NASCAR Cup Series was
held at the California Speedway on February 25, 2007,
and NASCAR Costner was chosen the official Grand
Marshal.In [66] He contributed to the production of the
2008 NASCAR documentary The Ride of Their Lives,
which was released in December, along with the
NASCAR Media Group and CMT Films. The
documentary's narrator would be Costner. He was also
chosen to serve as the spokesperson for May 15, 2009's
NASCAR Day. He would perform on the Charlotte
Motor Speedway infield the following day, May 16, and
serve as a judge for the 2nd annual Victory Challenge,
which took place prior to the 25th Running of the
NASCAR Sprint All-Star Race.

Writing

2015 saw Costner collaborate with John Baird,
researcher Stephen C. Meyer, illustrator Rick Ross, and

others on The Explorer's Guild: A Passage to Shambhala, a hybrid adventure/graphic novel.

Tim Ferriss's book Tools of Titans include a chapter by Costner that offers guidance.

CHAPTER 4: PERSONAL LIFE

Relationships

Costner began dating Cindy Silva, a fellow student, in 1975 while attending college; the two were married three years later. They had a son in 1988 and two daughters in 1984 and 1986 while they were married. After 16 years of marriage, the pair filed for divorce in 1994, purportedly as a result of Costner having an affair on the Waterworld set. A settlement of $80 million was given to Cindy Silva.

He briefly dated Bridget Rooney after his divorce, and the two of them had a son in 1996. After that, he dated Birgit Cunningham, a political activist. He shared a home with supermodel Elle Macpherson in 1996.

At his Aspen, Colorado ranch, on September 25, 2004, Costner tied the knot with Christine Baumgartner, a model and handbag designer, his girlfriend of four years. In addition to a daughter born in 2010, they have two sons born in 2007 and 2009. Baumgartner filed for divorce in May 2023. On September 19, 2023, their divorce was officially formalized.

Political Engagement

In his youth, Costner identified as a Republican. He was Ronald Reagan's friend and supporter, often going to golf with the former president. In the early 1990s, he changed his affiliation in the end. Costner has contributed to several Democratic politicians since 1992, such as Al Gore and Tom Daschle, although he has also contributed to Republican Phil Gramm as late as 1995.

He said in the open in 2008 that he had no desire to seek public office, adding, "I've lived quite a colorful life". Costner visited several locations in Colorado, where he owns a home, as part of his campaign for Barack Obama in the closing days leading up to that year's US presidential election. Costner emphasized in his speech the importance of young voters turning out to vote enthusiastically and early. At a demonstration held by Colorado State University, Costner declared, "We were going to change the world and we haven't". "My generation didn't get it done, and we need you to help us".

Costner thanked the British military fighting all across the world for their service in a commemorative letter written in October 2014.

At a rally in Indianola, Iowa, on December 22, 2019, Costner supported Democratic presidential candidate Pete Buttigieg. Subsequently, Costner backed Joe Biden, the Democratic nominee. A commercial for J. D. Scholten, a Democrat from Iowa's 4th congressional district seeking a seat in the U.S. House of Representatives, was narrated by Costner. Costner supported Republican Liz Cheney for reelection in the 2022 Wyoming US House of Representatives race.

CHAPTER 5: FILMOGRAPHY

In 1981, American actor, director, and producer Kevin Costner made his feature film debut in the romantic comedy Sizzle Beach, U.S.A. After that, he made appearances in the movies Testament (1983) and Shadows Run Black (1984) before starring with Kevin Kline, Scott Glenn, and Danny Glover in the ensemble western Silverado (1985). He co-starred with Judd Nelson in the comedy Fandango that same year. In the 1987 crime drama The Untouchables, starring Robert De Niro and Sean Connery, Costner played Eliot Ness. He co-starred with Tim Robbins and Susan Sarandon in the romantic comedy sports film Bull Durham the next year, playing the role of Crash Davis. The movie is listed in the AFI's Top 10 List of the Best Sports Films. After that, Costner and James Earl Jones starred in the sports fantasy drama film Field of Dreams. The movie was nominated for three Academy Awards, including Best Picture, Best Original Score, and Best Adapted Screenplay. Critics gave it largely excellent reviews. In

2017, the Library of Congress chose it as "culturally, historically, or aesthetically significant" and included it in the United States National Film Registry. It is also included in the AFI's list of the Top 10 Fantasy Films.

During the 1990s, Costner acted in a number of movies, including the epic Western Dances with Wolves (1990), which he also produced and directed. In that movie, he played Lieutenant John J. Dunbar. Costner won Best Picture, Best Director, and was nominated for Best Actor out of the twelve Academy Award nominations for the movie. Alongside Morgan Freeman, he played Robin Hood in Robin Hood: Prince of Thieves (1991), Whitney Houston in The Bodyguard (1992), Dennis Quaid in Wyatt Earp (1994), Rene Russo in Tin Cup (1996), Will Patton in The Postman (1997), Robin Wright in Message in a Bottle (1999), and Kelly Preston in For Love of the Game (1999). He costarred with Kurt Russell in the heist black action comedy 3000 Miles to Graceland (2001), with Robert Duvall in the Revisionist Western film Open Range (2003), with Jennifer Aniston in Rob Reiner's romantic comedy Rumor Has It (2005), with Demi

Moore in the psychological thriller Mr. Brooks (2007), and with Kelsey Grammer in the comedy-drama Swing Vote (2008).

In Zack Snyder's 2013 blockbuster movie Man of Steel, which was based on the DC Comics character Superman, he was chosen to play Jonathan Kent. He costarred with Chris Pine in Jack Ryan: Shadow Recruit (2014), Amber Heard in 3 Days to Kill (2014), and Jennifer Garner in Draft Day (2015). Costner received the Screen Actors Guild Award for Outstanding Performance by a Cast in a Motion Picture along with the rest of the cast for his performance in the 2016 biographical drama film Hidden Figures. In the 2017 biographical crime drama film Molly's Game, he portrayed Jessica Chastain's father. In the 2019 period crime thriller film The Highwaymen, he played lawman and Texas Ranger Frank Hamer, starring Woody Harrelson.

In the three-part Western television miniseries Hatfields & McCoys, Costner as Devil Anse Hatfield. Since 2018, he has been a cast member of Yellowstone, a neo-Western drama series, as John Dutton.

Movies Acted And Directed By Kelvin Costner

The early films of actor, director, and producer Kevin Costner in the 1980s and 1990s had a big influence. In "The Untouchables" (1987), he made his breakthrough as Eliot Ness, starring alongside a stellar ensemble. Costner's magnetism and austere demeanor hinted to his leading parts in the future.

After this triumph, Costner starred in the thriller "No Way Out" (1987), proving his versatility in a gripping film. But the 1989 film "Field of Dreams" cemented his place in the spotlight. Audiences were moved by the film's poignant tale, fantastical elements, and sports theme.

With "Dances with Wolves" (1990), Costner maintained his success. This movie not only marked his directorial debut but also brought him critical praise and multiple Academy Awards, including Best Picture and Best Director. The epic story of a soldier in the Civil War venturing into the Native American frontier demonstrated Costner's love of storytelling and dedication to his work.

Costner also demonstrated his versatility in the early 1990s by starring in "Robin Hood: Prince of Thieves" (1991) and "JFK" (1991). While "Robin Hood" demonstrated his abilities to helm a successful blockbuster, "JFK" showcased his work with filmmaker Oliver Stone in a drama with a strong political message.

These early motion pictures made Kevin Costner known as a captivating and adaptable actor who had a gift for choosing unusual parts that brought out his best qualities. The box office success of these films paved the way for his subsequent influence on the motion picture business.

Costner encountered both critical and financial difficulties in the mid-1990s due to his roles in movies such as "Waterworld" (1995) and "The Postman" (1997). Even with the financial disappointments, his willingness to take risks and pursue ambitious initiatives showed that he was committed to presenting stories that went beyond the norm.

In the sports comedy "Tin Cup" (1996), Costner played a broke golf pro. This marked Costner's comeback to popularity. The movie demonstrated his charming personality and aptitude for lighter fare. He co-starred with Whitney Houston in the romantic thriller "The Bodyguard" (1992), which not only cemented his reputation as a leading man but also showcased his extraordinary performance.

Throughout the late 1990s and early 2000s, Costner kept expanding the range of characters he played. He starred in romantic drama "Message in a Bottle" (1999) and historical drama "Thirteen Days" (2000) about the Cuban

Missile Crisis. These endeavors showcased his adaptability and eagerness to experiment with diverse genres.

Despite ups and downs in his career, Costner stayed a major player in Hollywood, playing everything from sports dramas like "McFarland, USA" (2015) to Westerns like "Open Range" (2003). His continued career in show business demonstrated not only his acting talent but also his versatility and resilience.

With his recent television successes, including the popular series "Yellowstone," Costner has garnered praise and established himself as a versatile artist in the entertainment business. In addition to laying the groundwork for his prosperous career, Kevin Costner's early roles demonstrated his adeptness in navigating the ever-changing Hollywood industry.

Kevin Costner kept making important contributions to television and movies in the 2010s. In the 2013 film "Man of Steel" directed by Zack Snyder, he played

Superman's adopted father, Jonathan Kent, lending gravitas to the superhero genre. This foray into the realm of blockbusters demonstrated his continuing popularity in a variety of cinema genres.

The 2012 television miniseries "Hatfields & McCoys" featured Costner in a pivotal role that brought him an Emmy Award for Outstanding Lead Actor. This achievement proved that he could move between large and small screens with ease, enhancing his reputation as a flexible actor.

His parts in the 2016 criminal drama "Hidden Figures" and the dramatic thriller "Criminal" further demonstrated his dedication to diverse storytelling. The way that "Hidden Figures" portrayed the African-American women mathematicians at NASA during the Space Race in particular won praise from critics.

Kevin Costner remained well-known throughout the 2020s, juggling his acting career with his love of music. He received a lot of appreciation for his role as the patriarch of a strong rancher family in the television series "Yellowstone," which helped to continue television's revival as a medium for excellent storytelling.

In addition to showcasing his acting prowess, Costner's long career also demonstrates his adaptability and perseverance in the face of a constantly changing entertainment industry. The cinema and television industries have been forever changed by Kevin Costner's contributions, from early triumphs to subsequent accomplishments.

In addition to pursuing his acting profession, Kevin Costner has increased his creative output in the last few years. Given that "Yellowstone" attracted a large audience due to its strong drama set against the backdrop of the American West, his role in the show has been especially important. The success of the show has been largely attributed to Costner's portrayal of John Dutton, the family patriarch.

Costner has continued to work as a filmmaker in addition to performing. The crime thriller "The Highwaymen" (2019) which followed the hunt for infamous robbers Bonnie and Clyde, starred and was directed by him. He was able to demonstrate his storytelling abilities in this dual capacity as actor and director, which also helped to revive interest in historical crime dramas.

Costner has also not lost sight of his love of music. His country music group, Kevin Costner & Modern West, is well-known; they have put out multiple CDs. His foray into the music business is evidence of his adaptability as a performer and his openness to experimenting with various media.

Kevin Costner is a seasoned and well-respected figure in the entertainment business, and his influence goes beyond his early roles. His status as a versatile talent has been cemented by his ability to adjust to shifting trends without sacrificing his dedication to excellent narrative, making him a long-lasting presence in both film and television.

Highlights Of Kevin Costner's Career

Kevin Costner is a well-known actor, producer, and director who has a noteworthy background. Starring parts in classic movies like "Dances with Wolves," for which he received the Academy Awards for Best Picture and Best Director, are among his career highlights. In addition, Costner became well-known for his roles in films such as "Robin Hood: Prince of Thieves," "Field of Dreams," and "The Bodyguard." His cross-genre adaptability has helped him establish himself as a major player in the entertainment business.

Apart from his achievements in movies, Kevin Costner has also made significant contributions to television. As the lead actor in the highly regarded miniseries "Hatfields & McCoys," he won a Primetime Emmy.

Costner's reputation as a reputable actor has been cemented by his ability to play interesting characters with nuance and honesty.

In addition to his playing career, Costner is a skilled producer and director of motion pictures. He directed and performed in "Dances with Wolves," a film that not only brought him an Academy Award, but also demonstrated his directing abilities. A number of popular movies have been made by his production firm, Tig Productions.

Costner's influence is not limited to the realm of athletics. His involvement in sports-themed movies such as "Field of Dreams" and "Bull Durham" is indicative of his love for the genre. Kevin Costner is a well-liked and enduring personality in the entertainment world thanks to his diverse career.

CHAPTER 6: KEVIN COSTNER HONORS AND AWARDS

Throughout his career, Kevin Costner, the well-known actor, producer, and director, has won numerous accolades. His two Academy Awards—one each for Best Picture and Best Director—for the 1990 picture "Dances with Wolves" are among his noteworthy accomplishments. Additionally, Costner has won three Golden Globes, one of which was for "Robin Hood: Prince of Thieves" (1991) as Best Actor in a Motion Picture Drama. He has also received numerous honors in recognition of his contributions to the entertainment sector.

Apart from his Golden Globes and Academy Awards, Kevin Costner has received accolades for his acting abilities and services to the movie business. The television miniseries "Hatfields & McCoys" (2012) won him a Primetime Emmy Award for Outstanding Lead Actor in a Miniseries or Movie.

In addition, Costner has won accolades including the American Film Institute's Lifetime Achievement Award in 2003 and the Silver Bear for Best Director at the Berlin International Film Festival for "Dances with Wolves". In addition to his brilliant playing career, he has left a lasting history in Hollywood as a producer and director of motion pictures. With his varied career and many awards, Costner has had a huge impact on the film industry.

Oscars Won By Kevin Costner

Notable success has been had by Kevin Costner at the Academy Awards. The movie "Dances with Wolves" (1990), in which he starred and directed, was his biggest success. Seven Oscars were won by the movie, including Best Picture and Best Director for Costner. The movie received high praise from critics. This was a turning point in his career that demonstrated both his acting and filmmaking prowess.

Costner's reputation in Hollywood has been cemented by his ability to move between directing and performing jobs with ease. His influence on the business was further highlighted by the Academy Award nomination, and "Dances with Wolves" continues to be a key role in his body of work. The Academy Awards were crucial in recognizing Costner's diverse abilities and accomplishments to the film industry.

In addition to "Dances with Wolves," Kevin Costner has had other noteworthy Academy Award experiences. For his performance in "Field of Dreams" (1989), he was nominated for another Oscar for Best Actor, demonstrating his ability to play a variety of personalities. Because of his performances, Costner has continuously received Academy Award nominations, demonstrating his continuing influence in the motion picture business.

Despite the fact that not all of Costner's films were well regarded by critics, his influence on the film industry is clear. His contributions to the field—both in front of and behind the camera—have made a significant impact that will never fade. He is a renowned figure in Hollywood thanks to the Academy Awards, which are a monument to his talent and the lasting impact he has made on the film industry.

Additional Awards for Kevin Costner

Apart from his triumph at the Academy Awards, Kevin Costner has received other accolades over his career. In 2003, he was awarded a star on the Hollywood Walk of Fame in appreciation for his services to the entertainment sector. His standing as a well-respected person in Hollywood is further cemented by this important award.

Costner's influence goes beyond accolades. In recognition of his ongoing impact on film, he received the Critics' Choice Movie Awards 2015 Lifetime Achievement Award. This recognition is a testament to his wider achievements as a producer, director, and filmmaker in addition to his standout performances.

In addition, his performance in the television miniseries "Hatfields & McCoys" brought him praise from critics and a Primetime Emmy Award, demonstrating his versatility in both film and television. These varied accolades highlight Kevin Costner's extensive and fruitful career in the entertainment business.

Beyond accolades, Kevin Costner's effect on the entertainment business is acknowledged for his cultural impact. He was honored in 2006 by the National Cowboy & Western Heritage Museum with his induction into the Western Performers Hall of Fame for his contributions to the Western genre, which were especially noticeable in movies such as "Dances with Wolves."

Nor has Costner's dedication to environmental problems gone ignored. For his efforts to increase public understanding of environmental issues, he was awarded the 1999 Global Environmental Citizen Award. This demonstrates his commitment to having a good influence outside of the entertainment industry.

Costner's achievements, which include environmental campaigning, cultural honors, and Hollywood acclaim, demonstrate a career that goes well beyond acting. His diverse contributions have had a lasting impact on many aspects of society.

CHAPTER 7 : LEGACY

Renowned actor, producer, and director Kevin Costner is well-known for his parts in classic movies like "Dances with Wolves," for which he received two Academy Awards. His contributions to great productions as a producer and director go well beyond his acting career. Costner's status as a diverse and powerful figure in the film industry has been cemented by his impact on it.

Apart from his achievements in the movie business, Kevin Costner has also had a significant impact as an entrepreneur and environmentalist. He is one of the co-founders of Ocean Therapy Solutions, a business that creates technologies to clean up oil spills. Costner's dedication to environmental problems is indicative of his ambition to have a good influence outside of the entertainment industry. This complex legacy demonstrates his adaptability and accomplishments beyond the screen as well.

In addition, Kevin Costner's resume spans a wide variety of genres, from the epic "Waterworld" to the timeless baseball picture "Field of Dreams." His adaptability to many roles has brought him great fame and a devoted following. In addition to his work in acting and environmental conservation, Costner's musical endeavors with his band, Kevin Costner & Modern West, demonstrate his love of creativity in a variety of artistic mediums and contribute yet another side to his rich legacy.

Enduring Influence

Kevin Costner's renowned appearances in films such as "Field of Dreams" and "Dances with Wolves" have had a lasting impression on the film industry. His contributions to the film landscape encompass both directing and acting.

Throughout his decades-long career, Kevin Costner has delivered adaptable performances in a variety of genres.

In addition to bringing him praise, his performance as Lt. Dunbar in "Dances with Wolves" changed how people saw Native American culture in movies. With the same picture, Costner made his directing debut and won many Oscars, showcasing his versatility.

Ever since it captured the spirit of dreams, athletics, and father-son interactions, "Field of Dreams" has remained a classic. Audiences have been forever impacted by Costner's on-screen persona and commitment to storytelling, which has added to the rich cultural fabric of American cinema.

Kevin Costner went on to make important contributions to film after his initial achievements. He became a major Hollywood actor in the 1990s with his roles in big-budget films like "Robin Hood: Prince of Thieves" and "The Bodyguard." His flexibility was demonstrated by his ability to move across genres with ease, from romantic thrillers to historical dramas.

With portrayals as real players in movies like "Bull Durham" and "For Love of the Game," Costner had an impact on the sports genre as well. His dedication to portraying characters as authentically as possible struck a chord with viewers, making him a dependable and lucrative celebrity.

With standout roles in shows like "Man of Steel" and "Yellowstone," Costner's career saw a rebirth in the twenty-first century, proving his continuing appeal to audiences of all ages. His impact on the entertainment industry is significant since it goes beyond his acting career and includes his work as a producer and director.

Influence On Cinema

Kevin Costner's many roles and achievements as an actor, director, and producer have had a tremendous impact on film. His roles in classic movies like "Dances with Wolves" and "Field of Dreams" demonstrated his talent for giving characters nuance and realism, winning him praise from critics and changing the narrative landscape in the business. Costner's influence as a director is clear from his work on "Dances with Wolves," which took home multiple Oscars, including Best Picture and Best Director. All things considered, his work has had a significant impact on the film industry.

Kevin Costner's impact on film goes beyond his accomplishments as an actor and director; he also played a significant role in creating particular genres. His work on iconic sports movies like "Field of Dreams" and "Bull Durham" helped reshape sports narrative by placing an emphasis on interpersonal relationships and emotional depth rather than just competitiveness.

Costner's versatility across multiple genres, ranging from historical epics to modern dramas, played a part in the development of leading males in Hollywood. His charisma on TV and common sense appeal struck a chord with viewers in the latter half of the 20th century, making him a highly sought-after performer.

In addition, Costner's influence is noteworthy due to his dedication to films with compelling themes and societal significance. He was eager to work with historically significant narratives in movies like "JFK" and "Thirteen Days," which gave mainstream film a more contemplative edge.

In addition to his starring career, Costner's forays into producing have cemented his influence in the business. His production business, Tig Productions, was involved in presenting productions that reflected his love of narrative and frequently embraced an Americana aesthetic.

To put it simply, Kevin Costner's diverse contributions to the film industry have had a lasting impact on both the artistic and commercial facets of the motion picture industry. Not only can his influence be seen in specific performances, but it can also be seen in the more general patterns and methods of narrative that arose during his significant years in Hollywood.

Kevin Costner's engagement in large-scale, ground-breaking projects is another way that he has impacted cinema. "Waterworld," in spite of its early difficulties, demonstrated his readiness to embark on audacious and creative ideas, stretching the limits of cinematography. Despite some negative reviews, the film's production value and concept permanently altered Hollywood's method of crafting expansive, post-apocalyptic settings.

A second example of Costner's ability to bring old stories to life was his performance in "Robin Hood: Prince of Thieves," which helped spark a trend of medieval-themed movies in the early 1990s. His interpretation of the well-known figure demonstrated his range and gave the historical adventure genre a contemporary twist.

Furthermore, Costner's influence may be seen in his partnerships with other notable figures in the industry. His relationship with filmmaker Ron Shelton on movies such as "Bull Durham" and "Tin Cup" not only elevated sports-themed films to a new level but also underscored the significance of character-driven tales, setting an example for fruitful partnerships in the business.

Storytelling was always Costner's passion, even as Hollywood changed. Later parts in movies such as "The Highwaymen" showed him to be able to change with the times and still stay true to stories that delve into the intricacies of the human condition.

To put it simply, Kevin Costner's impact on film extends beyond his individual roles; it also includes his willingness to take chances, work on a variety of genres, and contribute to the narrative and visual advancement of the genre over time.

CHAPTER 8: BEHIND THE SCENES OF KEVIN COSTNER

Renowned producer, director, and actor Kevin Costner is best recognized for his work in the motion pictures "Dances with Wolves" and "The Bodyguard." He regularly participates in filmmaking behind the scenes, frequently producing and occasionally directing his own works. In addition, Costner has a band named Kevin Costner & Modern West since he loves music so much. He has also engaged in a number of business endeavors, such as a collaboration with a technology firm that specializes in the remediation of oil spills. Costner has had a varied career in front of and behind the camera, which is influenced by his wide range of interests.

Aside from his contributions to the entertainment business, Kevin Costner's affinity for the American West is evident in a lot of his movie selections. His feature film debut, "Dances with Wolves," demonstrated his dedication to real storytelling while also garnering him critical praise and multiple accolades.

Costner's participation in the post-apocalyptic movie "Waterworld" was noteworthy due to the difficulties encountered during production in addition to the film's enormous budget. Through the years, the movie has developed a cult following despite early failures and negative reviews.

Aside from performing and directing movies, Costner is a passionate sports fan. A minor league baseball team he owns and the baseball-themed film "Field of Dreams" are just two of the sports-related endeavors he has been involved in.

Despite the highs and lows of his career, Costner's continued success in the business is a testament to his adaptability and love of presenting stories in a variety of formats and genres. Kevin Costner continues to be a well-known personality in the entertainment industry, both on film and off.

Kevin Costner, Producing And Directing

In addition to becoming a well-known actor, Kevin Costner has also shown his versatility in the film industry by dabbling in directing and producing. "Dances with Wolves," a historical epic that won seven Academy Awards, including Best Picture and Best Director for Costner, marked his directorial debut in 1990.

After this triumph, Costner pursued his directing career with movies like "Open Range" (2003) and "The Postman" (1997). Even though these movies had mixed reviews, they showed how interested he was in investigating other storytelling styles and genres.

With his production firm, TIG Productions, Costner has produced a number of different projects. His productions include the box office hits "Robin Hood: Prince of Thieves" (1991) and "Bodyguard" (1992).

Costner is not limited to traditional theater cinema in his engagement in filmmaking. He has contributed to and supported environmental technology projects, especially those that deal with cleaning up oil spills. This demonstrates his wider passions and dedication to changing the world for the better outside of the entertainment industry.

In conclusion, Kevin Costner's contributions to producing and directing highlight his varied involvement in influencing the storylines of movies, ranging from being in front of the camera to assuming creative authority behind it.

The Hollywood Impact Of Kevin Costner

In his roles as an actor and director, Kevin Costner has made a big impact on Hollywood. Over the course of his decades-long career, a number of factors have contributed to his influence:

1. Actor Versatility: Costner's ability to move between multiple genres with ease, from historical dramas like "Dances with Wolves" to sports pictures like "Bull Durham" and "Field of Dreams," demonstrated his versatility and made him a highly sought-after leading man.

2. Directorial Success: Costner's "Dances with Wolves," his directing debut, brought him multiple Academy Awards, including Best Director, in addition to critical acclaim. His accomplishment validated his skills as a filmmaker and helped Hollywood acknowledge actors who became filmmakers.

3. Box Office Success: Costner has starred in a number of highly profitable motion pictures, including "Waterworld," "Robin Hood: Prince of Thieves," and "The Bodyguard." His involvement in these films

frequently resulted in box office success, enhancing his reputation as a bankable star.

4. Cultural Impact: Movies such as "The Bodyguard" and "Field of Dreams" have had a long-lasting effect on culture. These films' lines, sequences, and even the soundtrack have endured and grown iconic in the eyes of viewers.

5. Dedication to Real Storytelling: Costner's commitment to real storytelling, which is most clear in "Dances with Wolves," has inspired a new wave of filmmakers to value sincere storylines and a range of viewpoints.

6. Entrepreneurial Ventures: Costner's business endeavors, particularly his investments in environmental technology, demonstrate a larger connection with social and technological issues and enhance his reputation in Hollywood. This goes beyond his roles as actor and director.

Despite difficulties and ups and downs throughout his career, Kevin Costner's ongoing presence—both on and off screen—reflects a long-lasting influence on the Hollywood scene. His contributions to the entertainment world as an actor, director, and businessman are irreversible.

In addition, Kevin Costner's influence on Hollywood is seen in his production work. He has worked on a number of concepts that have been brought to the big screen via his production business, TIG Productions. This includes financially successful movies like "Robin Hood: Prince of Thieves," which emphasized his influence behind-the-scenes as well as his acting abilities.

It's impressive how keen Costner is to take on challenging tasks. "Waterworld," in spite of difficulties encountered during production and conflicting reviews, proved his dedication to pushing the limits of cinema. The movie's lasting impact has changed over time, and it continues to be evidence of Costner's willingness to take artistic chances.

Apart from conventional Hollywood productions, Costner's participation in sports-oriented films like "Bull Durham" and "Field of Dreams" added to the appeal of the genre and showcased his capacity to engage viewers through diverse cinematic encounters.

Furthermore, Costner's impact goes beyond the big screen. His commitment to environmental causes, especially in the area of oil spill cleanup technology development, demonstrates a socially conscience side that fits well with changing industry trends. His dedication to environmental concerns establishes him as a prominent Hollywood personality involved in wider societal issues.

In conclusion, Kevin Costner has had a wide-ranging influence on Hollywood thanks to his work as an advocate, director, producer, and actor. In the entertainment sector, his ability to work across genres, take on challenging projects, and address social and environmental issues has had a lasting impact.

CHAPTER 9:CONCLUSION

Thoughts On An Amazing Career

The variety of Kevin Costner's career is evident in his classic parts in films such as "Dances with Wolves" and "The Bodyguard." His versatility in genres is a testament to his amazing journey through Hollywood's ever-changing scene, making a lasting impression on viewers everywhere.

Over several decades, Costner's career in Hollywood has demonstrated his abilities as both a director and an actor. With roles in films such as "Robin Hood: Prince of Thieves" and "Field of Dreams," as well as the massive box office triumph of "Dances with Wolves," for which he received numerous Oscars, Costner's on-screen persona has come to represent the pinnacle of cinematic greatness.

Beyond acting, he has a strong sense of narrative, as seen in his directing endeavors such as "Open Range" and "The Postman". His love of athletics is reflected in Costner's dedication to his projects, as shown in the movies "Bull Durham" and "For Love of the Game."

Costner's lasting popularity in a field characterized by ephemeral trends stems from his ability to engage viewers in a variety of genres. Whether he's playing a contemporary bodyguard, a wanderer from the future, or a baseball star, his performances are memorable and add to the history that characterizes Hollywood's golden age. The entertainment industry as a whole is impacted by Costner, whose influence goes beyond the big screen. His commitment to realism in parts such as Eliot Ness in "The Untouchables" and Jim Garrison in "JFK" shows a passion for storytelling that goes beyond acting.

In the mid-1990s, Costner took on the difficult task of both producing and acting in "Waterworld," a movie that was frequently beset by difficulties during production but demonstrated his desire to push limits anyway. Even though the movie received a mixed response, Costner's willingness to venture into unknown areas demonstrates his sense of adventure.

Projects like "Yellowstone" have re-established him in the public eye in recent years, demonstrating that his capacity to demand attention has not diminished with age. Because of his genuineness, which elevates him above the status of an actor and leaves a lasting impression on the annals of cinematic honesty, Costner has endured as a popular figure in the history of film.

The Status Of Kevin Costner In Cinema History

In movie history, Kevin Costner is largely remembered for his work in the latter half of the 20th century. His parts in classic movies like "Dances with Wolves," for which he received Best Picture and Best Director Oscars, helped him rise to fame. Through his successful acting career spanning multiple genres, Costner helped shape the cinematic landscape in the 1980s and 1990s.

Beyond just acting, Costner has had a significant influence in Hollywood thanks to his successful directing roles in films like "Dances with Wolves," which highlighted his talent for narrative. His participation in sports movies such as "Field of Dreams" and "Bull Durham" enhanced his reputation as a filmmaker and encapsulated the essence of American culture. Despite setbacks in his career, Costner's legacy as an actor and director will always be felt in the film industry.

Kevin Costner's star power contributed to the success of blockbuster films like "The Bodyguard" and "Robin Hood: Prince of Thieves," in addition to his acting and directing. His flexibility was demonstrated by his on-screen charisma and ability to play a variety of characters, including dramas and Westerns. Costner is an important character in the complex fabric of film history because of his lasting influence on Hollywood, even in the face of the industry's constant change.

Some motivation quotes from Kevin Costner

1. "I'm not a guy who's afraid of commitment. I'm not afraid of saying, 'Yes, this is what I want.'"

2. "I believe people who go into politics want to do the right thing. And then they hit a big wall of re-election and the pettiness of politics. In the end, it's not about winning in the next election. It's about doing the right thing."

3. "I think that inside every adult is the heart of a child. We just gradually convince ourselves that we have to act more like adults."
4. "Success is something you experience when you act accordingly. Success is not something you have, it's something you do."

These quotes reflect Costner's perspective on commitment, the balance between adulthood and inner child, and the proactive nature of success.

SEVERAL KEVIN COSTNER MOVIES

Kevin Costner has acted in a lot of movies. "Dances with Wolves," "The Bodyguard," "Field of Dreams," and "Robin Hood: Prince of Thieves" are a few that stand out.

Of course! Kevin Costner's career has been varied, encompassing a number of genres. He also starred in the post-apocalyptic adventure "Waterworld" and the sports romance comedy "Tin Cup," in addition to the previously mentioned movies. Both "JFK" and "The Untouchables" exemplify his work in the political thriller genre and crime drama. In "Man of Steel," another movie in Costner's resume, he played Jonathan Kent in the DC Extended Universe.

"The Postman," a dystopian thriller, and "Open Range," a Western that he also directed, are among Kevin

Costner's films. He was a major character in the superhero movie "Batman v. Superman: Dawn of Justice." In addition, Costner acted in two films: "No Way Out," a political thriller, and "Message in a Bottle," a romantic drama. His varied parts add to a broad, multi-decade career in film.

In summary, "Kevin Costner" offers an engrossing examination of the celebrated actor's life and career. The book goes into great detail about Costner's career, covering everything from his enduring appearances in classic movies to his influence on the entertainment business. Readers come away from it knowing more about the real man who created the characters and his lasting impact on Hollywood.

The story recounts not just Costner's ascent to fame but also the obstacles he encountered and surmounted during his professional life. The book highlights Costner's range as an actor, from the grand epics of "Dances with Wolves" to the poignant performances in films like "Field of Dreams."

It also explores his activities outside of performing, like his directing endeavors and producing work. These chapters highlight Costner's many accomplishments to the film business, highlighting his impact as a creative force and his commitment to narrative.

The examination of Costner's private life, with all of its highs and lows, gives the story a more relatable edge. By comprehending the intricacies that influenced his path, readers are able to acquire a deeper picture of the man behind the scenes. With its masterful portrayal of Kevin Costner, the book gives readers a deep respect for his accomplishment in film as well as a feeling of intimacy with the man beneath the fame.